María Baranda was born in Mexico City in 1962. Among her many prizes are two FONCA "young artist" fellowships in poetry, a FONCA/Rockefeller nonfiction fellowship the National Efraín Huerta, the Aguascalientes National Poetry Prize, the Villa de Madrid Latin American Poetry Prize of Madrid, Spain, and the FILIJ Children's Story Prize.

She is the author of more than a dozen books of poetry and eight works of children's literature. Her poems have been translated into English, French, Lithuanian, and German. In the U.S., her poems have appeared in *Chicago Review, Zoland Poetry, Boston Review, Circumference, Washington Square,* and in the anthologies *Connecting Lines: New Poetry from Mexico* (Sarabande Books) and *Reversible Monuments: Contemporary Mexican Poetry* (Copper Canyon Press).

~

Joshua Edwards was born in Galveston, Texas. He publishes and co-edits Canarium Books and, on occasion, *The Canary*. His own poems have appeared in *Colorado Review, CROWD, Slate, Verse, Vanitas, The Literary Review, Court Green, PRACTICE,* and elsewhere. He is currently a Stegner fellow at Stanford University and lives in Berkeley with his partner, the poet and translator Lynn Xu.

By María Baranda in Spanish

El jardín de los encantamientos (1990)
Fábula de los perdidos (1990)
Ficción de cielo (1995)
Los memoriosos (1995)
Moradas imposibles (1998)
Nadie, los ojos (1999)
Atlántica y el rústico (2002)
Dylan y las ballenas (2003)
Ávido mundo (2005)
Ficticia (2006)
Ávido mundo (2008) (Selected Poems)

As editor
Anuario de poesía mexicana 2008 (with Tedi López-Mills)

Ficticia

MARÍA BARANDA

*Translated from Spanish by
Joshua Edwards*

Shearsman Books
Exeter

This translation first published in the United Kingdom in 2010 by
Shearsman Books Ltd
58 Velwell Road
Exeter EX4 4LD

www.shearsman.com

ISBN 978-1-84861-123-8
First Edition

Original poems copyright © María Baranda, 2006.
Translations copyright © Joshua Edwards, 2010.

The right of María Baranda to be identified as the author
of this work, and of Joshua Edwards to be identified as the
translator thereof, has been asserted by them in accordance
with the Copyrights, Designs and Patents Act of 1988.
All rights reserved.

Cover: 'A Wave' by Van Edwards.

Acknowledgements

Excerpts from *Ficticia* first appeared in *Action Yes, Chicago Review, Circumference, Hayden's Ferry Review, Northwest Review, turnrow, Washington Square,* and *Zoland Poetry.* Thanks to the editors.

Thanks also to Luis Amador, Patricia Mendoza and Lynn Xu for their enthusiasm and support, and to Kent Johnson and Gustavo Fricke who provided invaluable suggestions and helped shape many of these translations.

This translation was supported by a Fulbright-García Robles Grant and a Vermont Studio Center Zoland Fellowship. Much gratitude to everyone who made those gifts of time possible, especially Roland Pease of Zoland Books and Gary Clark of Vermont Studio Center.

Most of all, a million thanks to María Baranda for graciously allowing me to translate her wonderful book.

Contents

I	[Everything begins with the moon and a desolate sky]	7
II	[You believe there are hummocks of ice outside]	9
III	[Rats devour your tongue]	11
IV	[You dream you're a Hindu in an intolerable jungle]	13
V	[When you were a child trees yielded in your path]	15
VI	[It was the time in which Mutis ordered a metropolis]	17
VII	[Domestic silence. Sailboats.]	19
VIII	[Saints stabbed at daybreak. Blunders.]	21
IX	[The voice of your ancestors was a single word]	23
X	[I ask for rain. I claim all sand for myself]	25
XI	[It is a fragmented truth that the hills point to]	27
XII	[The Consul has arrived with a desire to stampede in the summer]	29
XIII	*Letters to Robinson*	31
XIV	[We will never know paradise]	49
XV	[And we will descend to other violent rivers]	51
XVI	*Sky Cycle*	53
XVII	[I see you now, in your crust of light and song, at the earthy]	78

I

Everything begins with the moon and a desolate sky,
a place of frail words to open
the native prose of dreams. Calm
country poplars, Indian laurels
rise up, anxious on this island of memory.
There go the men who sail into port
when the word burns like a suburb
of truth, a mark on the page
that formed the earth. They approach too quickly.
They have lost the light and now break open a sea curd
in which time crackles.
They want to erase their names, to plant scams
in slow spirals of foam.
They recite a verse in an exiled country
like a clear net around infinite oceans.
There is blood between the rocks.
You listen to them. You wait for their silence.
You know they constitute an era.
Who will defend them from themselves?
Who will endure their eternal burden,

their first night of wind?
They'll remain in books forever.
Syllables of gratitude, sentences where the remnants
of their century glimmer.
They are a sliver of light within the atlas of time.
You pray for them.
You open a coconut and you drink from it.
Bells ring where birds chirp,
where fish throb with the calmness
of a heart that's on its own.
Once again the dream flows beneath your palm-thatched hut.
Who delights in you? Who says such prayers for you?
You imagine a period as your cry's spell.
You say that spring waits
in each of your own flood's hollows.
And in your smile. You know it's all a mistake.
A small part where you dissolve
into nature. You resist fear
with a tender secret.
There is a child in your bed. Keep quiet.

II

You believe there are hummocks of ice outside.
You dream of the Hilton's air conditioning,
of the brief appearance of a luxurious dish
that someone brings to your room while you
listen to the sea in the drain.
You need nobody.
You prefer to stroll along your boulevard
of skyscrapers and palm trees.
A broken transmitter's sound
hangs in the air.
It's a crab.
On this side of the coast you hope to see women
moving toward you
in a moment of calm or of ebb and flow.
You listen to the commotion of invisible docks.
The flesh of sailors that peels off like bark.
Someone wipes a trace of sweat from your cheek.
A halo of voices floods the secret creatures.
You're tired of their sounds.
They are your heart's deceptions,

your hands' lines
begging for a morsel of truth and nothing more.
You resist the desire to be one with time.
You know that at least some justice must rain
down upon your neighborhood of sand.
Wholeness is a bellflower open
to the insect's offices,
the trough of truth and mercy
where nobody can refuse
a spent life's waste.
Pity, you say, pity for such recklessness.
And you're overjoyed.

III

Rats devour your tongue.
Now you cry out for sorrow.
That terrible feeling trapped
in your grandmother's plastic curtains.
You root around in her ruins. There's nothing.
She died some time ago
with a girl's syphilis.
Her rocking chair is still
on the porch of that home in Texas.
At the gate there's a blue handkerchief
to guard against suspicion.
Nobody even gives it a second look. Sepia photos
of a cheap butcher shop
in the mist's gullet.
Endless words. Glassware.
And you want to guard the alphabets
of those who defend
your illegitimate name
inside a war's crags and rocks.
You try vertigo and levitation so that

the world revolves in its own emptiness.
Genuflections. Keepers of splendor
written with ink that multiplies
every vigil's quiet rumor. Such is its destiny.
Exile is a blank sheet of Bible paper
where the world traces its apocryphal limits,
its cries of truth and madness.
Peace, peace for the deer and leopard,
peace for that giver of life.
Every echo is part of the rubble
that we all collect.
Pieces of paradise. Any island
is the bat's playground,
its region of identity, dominion
where salt's pardon takes shelter.
Crossroads and detours.
Signs announce the defeated in Latin.
Cables that remind you of streets
lost in a vague geography.
There are no hours. Mankind's tick tock is emptied
by pronouncements of unhappiness. There is no pain.

IV

You dream you're a Hindu in an intolerable jungle.
You see birds falling at daybreak.
And you proclaim them.
You say they are all your daughters.
You are the son of a shy beauty,
the one who undresses at night
in front of the fig tree's captive cutting edge.
You confuse your age with heaven's limits.
You think the sea is only one more battle
from victory over the rain and its insistence.
Something makes you think of Ocosingo
and the indigenous in their white robes.
You cannot sing in another language.
The tribes of Virgil's dreams
are for you a boundary,
the unbroken dominion of permanence.
You see them pass in line like cardboard soldiers,
butterflies from high desert that unravel
the lightning. Moons from other skies.
A fish tells you about the depiction of a lonesome death.

Someone without their own portion of dawn.
You cover their nakedness.
Such is happiness: to think that outside
there is always the vertigo of some face
that waits for us.
You have seen the sun dally in a grain of sand.
You have heard the soft voice of a girl
undress for you like a calm dog
resting between pages of Homer.
Endless passages where someone makes a story
from a metal fragment and a swatch of fog
in the dry prairie of a few fire lines.
Refined calcium traces in your golden kitchen.
Visits from salt and its proverbs
like a single wound so that you
can make an apocryphal thought of your island.

V

When you were a child trees yielded in your path.
Night was a lantern in a palace of lilies.
You wanted to possess the cloak of every secret,
the days' briefest light
and the sword of truth as a silhouette.
You could have been an ideal Lancelot,
or maybe a Robin Hood
in the empire of tears.
You walk these dried out roads
that called for the sun to make a corpse of you,
a blind child of God
who grows accustomed to navigating
beneath a thorny sky.
You come to a halt in Van Gogh's shadow.
You rust.
You shout for some peace
from that ocean of burning purpose.
You throw yourself into it. Like that verse from Vallejo
that Elisio Diego kept in his head.
It was a pelican.

A song that was left in the furious
and definitive waters of children.
And you also ask who.
Who appears between you and mystery.
The poet's lost throne.
Your privilege is to search for lures
in the printed lines of life.

VI

It was the time in which Mutis ordered a metropolis.
He wanted a place for a top man.
We looked for the energy of Keats
and the stars' invincible chatter.
We wanted a time of rest and relaxation.
We imagined earth's pulse,
the exact dimension of all geometry
that in day and night would help us find
the limits of each century's asphalt.
There was somebody guarding birthrights
like a place for separating out
the machines of solitude from the racket
of someone getting up to take shelter in madness
in the middle of the night.
The city, then, protected us
as if in a frame of long old shadows,
fierce sustenance for the always lonely.
The dead were everyone else's dead,
tails of a coin
that didn't flip for us.

Helmets, helmets, checkpoints of a fate
that pulled apart pride.
There was a Jesuit who traveled through the jungle
and discovered amber and coal, the broken up
place of the mestizo.
And we were world. World like an ingot of gold.
World of a paradise that erupted into history.
Shells at dusk.
Feathers that disappeared in the Atlas range.

VII

Domestic silence. Sailboats.
Valleys that declare
a god's collapse in the desert. Deceptions.
The skin's dictations in a world of smoke.
Places for invocation and prayer.
Heads that surround their tongues' malice
as if they were insects beneath
summer's lost foam.
Numbers in the mouth of distant delights
where mankind is dust. We are.
City of tunnels and maps, murdered by a sun
that kneels before the pages of its literature.
Coffers of stupidity and emptiness, trucks
that move in silence down highways
until a tremendous warning, a cry
announces the new impulse of faith and desertion.
Combatants humming behind their guns. Testimonies.
Dawns cracked by military motivation.
Mud sanctuaries for the sibyl's mirror, darkness,
darkness for the soliloquy of nighttime parasites.

Faces. Replicas. Airborne eggshells
that humble a birdcall's majesty.
Bodies asleep in the half-light of their bedroom
as if they were moss, fossils in the sobriety
of whomever asked a favor of smoke's eyes.
Ancient visions.
Parts of a world that broke apart in the pillow.
Who has left us with empty arms?
Jeremiah speaks at the wall, his wall of a thousand lamentations,
collapses and falls silent. John cries in his invisible river,
his water of salt and baptism. The nightingale loses its voice
and the chameleon with its virtue of being reflected into
    reflection
tumbles down in the afternoon's brilliance.
Can it be that nobody sees, that nobody hears anymore?

VIII

Saints stabbed at daybreak. Blunders.
Wherever you go beware of sacrifices.
Don't allow them to pull your heart up into the sky,
to tear up your circle of light
and splendor with their shrapnel.
Deputies of moss and noise,
they roar in the heat and recant.
Let's speak of salt
and its morning puzzles.
Verses, verses that carry you
to valleys and farms.
Places grown old
from the desolation of a purposeless pen.
Choirs of birds that make your eyes heavy.
Women who write with the boredom of men
like the grimace of contradiction and consequence.
Sunday rhymes. Grumbling beneath the frond
of a story awoke the titans.
You design a dry word's harmony between
your sandy syllables. And you do nothing else.

You can no longer tremble before the mirror
of such false proclamations.
Broken images of a girl in the sea
and the warbling of a bird in water.
You paint the horizon blue
beneath the rain's perspiring flowers.
There are trees dressed in red and purple.
Blood in the province of a land
that was for you a part of your name,
your visions' orphaned condition.
Always remember the taste of plum.
The history that resounds in Welsh drums
and a Caribbean bay where you dreamed of light
and its infinite dog race around the world.
You could never love in a foreign language.

IX

The voice of your ancestors was a single word:
home. Domestically the buds,
the trees pruned into strange shapes.
A town's roads formed Sunday.
It was always January in family albums.
One single step to say: home.
Chandeliers and brass trays. Fine china.
Dishes of a gullible Pole who protects
cream and salt as if they where integral to her life.
Letters from new eras. Telegrams that would open
the basket of stories, places for burying relatives.
Shadows of pale children who never arrived.
Voices in the streets divided by echoes
from a new and tentative culture. Whispers.
Families of sermons, priests that would twist their voices
into children's throats.
In the rain, we took our seats alongside serenity.
Branches were bent back as in a Turner painting.
We had to learn the games of a fish
who peddled with the accent "Meester, meester, a dime?"

Hissing that rested in a tree of departed prepositions.
Aunts painted with a first pregnancy's bubbling,
cousins who ruined our dreams of false delights,
of wooden positions in a forest of assorted climates.
How many types of trees arrived from that coast.
You, with an alphabet of other assertions,
ask for a world in each eye
a reflection of identical, perpetual light.

X

I ask for rain. I claim all sand for myself.
Whitewashing waves and waves in a sea of thorns.
Rivers that hem me in, nautical passions,
trees with greasy bark and false crowns,
flames in the sky above a burning forest.
Drones. Crags.
Who scattered the sea's voice
as if it were the sky?
Who said that flying
was waiting for blood's fire,
the wind's most vigorous heart?
I wanted a plane,
an arrow that would spread me through the clouds
quickly, anonymously, and silently.
I wanted to fly.
Fighting injustice, the shadow's gamble,
the open ash of wings.
I was free to live by the insect's
compass in water's folds.
At that time the countryside

meant the smell of my thirteen years,
the gutter open at gates of exile
and grace.
Abrupt pen in the announcement of individuality,
booming light of lightning
during a feverish night of extinct storms.
I cannot recover that fable
lost to old paradises, the inaccessible
first time I learned my voice could be my cry.
I have lost myself to the wall of my limitations.
I look for shade on a balcony in faraway tropics,
a coast open to desires
and a blue promise scribbled
in an old black notebook to my grandfather:
I will write on the crack.
Now I'm staggering through the footprints
of my years in a stuttering garden,
among ruins, old enchantments.

XI

for Juan Carvajal

It is a fragmented truth that the hills point to,
a cracking of lime and pride
in the empire of iguana and viper.
It is rain that falls in a time of other wars,
battles won by thought,
hieroglyphs from different languages.
And on the freshly wet terrace,
Juan invokes Seferis as a way
to overcome our sadness.
Temples of an ocean concocted in his library,
Helens lost to those who couldn't see them.
A boat arrives at our beach.
Patroclus comes ashore with his dispossessed tongue.
There is a shovel in the ground and a question that ends up
as an echo of this Mediterranean gray
that hid in a Cuernavacan garden.
We were eternal.
Definitive between the errant syllables of the friend
who translated a world
and its void for us.

Is there a privilege for having heard
this athletic Quasimodo
who broke apart the ancient alphabet
and its August reflections?
What child was in those boxcars
of salt and remorse?
Which is the song of the men
who shake before an epithet
and get sick in the presence of a precise syllable?
Lines of light rise up
as if they were virgins, vipers
of an age when the sea was a resting place.

XII

The Consul has arrived with a desire to stampede in the summer.
Arrived with a blue jacket and the self-confidence
of someone who wants to die beneath the extinguished smoke
of a mud and putty volcano. Pretense in pieces.
Ancient avenues where harmony is inlaid
between tattered old socks.
And a challenge from the void shakes us all:
Why the hurry? Sparrows from other mountains
come to see, to watch for a delayed interior,
a fragment of the brotherhood that burned in the cantina.
Streets of a Cuauhnáhuac that no longer exists, time
of other statues in parks and gardens where nobody
never is forever no more. Handicrafts of an already
dissolved senate, shops for judges and their cloned
voices, palates of extinct silverware.
Songs of inelegant men who find their menial
whip in generations of snow.
Castaways from other small territories that come here
like cadavers with neither peace nor testament. Empty streets,
hotels where cats are martyrs damned by rats.

Old distilleries, places for the foreigner's dance
and his visitations, dreams to continue the search
for some more grace and deception. Fresh fragrances,
heartbroken dogs like those in Aeschylus's baths.
And those of us who held life in our hands,
we were unable to live aboard that drunken boat that set sail
for new courses with uncanny composure.

XIII
(Letters to Robinson)

i

We heard the heron at the end of July.
It had come to sing with a solitary quack
of oceanic time and an uncertain and speechless
dream of girls, the dry voice of wind and distance.
Dark secrets of goodness. False visions
beneath this soil. Alphabets that herald
the cleaner letters of abyss.
The lookout of sweat has arrived
like a verb's shadow.
Where we speak of domestic things,
shattered glass, mirrors for the faces
of who we never were,
always leaves us behind.
Now we see a thousand faces immersed
in mundane files
of loneliness and doubt,
records for the crystal ball of apparitions.
Subtle features that never changed

us into a precise feline print.
Time dragged along
by the salt of a world
that never belonged to us.
Now that we rest our delirium
beneath a whitewashed sky we can desecrate
the secrets held by men of a never-ending
history: destiny's
small disciples. Women in the midst of absence,
places distinguished by a lack of rain,
liquors for the insomnia of those who didn't die.

Now that the light has been put out like a trace
of initial infancy, a lone crack
in our lives, we can travel with a lost bird's
invitation, with the winged idea
we once believed it ignited.

Now nothing is in the face of the wind: not the tinted verb
of familiar adolescence, nor that childhood
guarded by the beast in its jars of alcohol and prophecy.
Nor that adolescence of the princes of Eden,
kings of a paradise within an inescapable hole.

Now we can lick our trophies, the exact division
of a mask-filled forest that made us
into soldiers for a story without end or beginning.

ii

Robinson you failed. Your mind was changed
into a vain mirage of disenchantments.
I'll no longer look after your home, that small den
where rain could undo the stink
of proverbs and relics.
I'll no longer watch over your cave of salt and bread
where the scorpion's peace
is your measured anger's kingdom.
You will remain as stubborn as a shark waiting
for small prey. I'll watch you with doubt,
not knowing if you're on your way to a world already sunk
in the hot night of empty hands.
Or if you advance toward the walls of time
like a dream in which you believe you're exhaling
the savage nature of secret things.
Here I will be able to listen to your crying,
your bright and womanly flame, your pride
of a bird plunging into rotten water.

Come, Robinson, approach the garden of other delights.
Now your planet, that small territory where
your name collected the weight of the chosen, is strange.
Be dazzled by the seagull's cry.
You will no longer perish, there will no longer be moon and sun
roots to preserve the thirst of those who love alone.

iii

Gardens of an arrested time in the window.
Bitter forecasts. Winters eroded
in the salt from a door of light and glass.
I am not mistaken.
I know sand's dreamscapes are sad,
the tracks we leave little by little
like a landscape tattooed on the skin of insomniacs.
The chairs of time that once supported the figure
of a farmer sowing in rain are broken.
Once again it was Virgil and his severed pledge,
whitecaps as old as the forest floor,
boars and lionesses yoked together and an immense
half-pruned elm that stayed like this with the power
of the dead Latin in your notebooks.
Conquered are the rocking chairs
where we rock a dead child back and forth
to the coo of mother vipers,
mother snakes, mothers without mothers,

orphans of delirium, and in that tepid bunk
we could hide tributes of dust and ash.
Domestic Robinson, computer of lives
and soliloquies, grinder of promises
in pages upon pages of your literature.
I've watched you meditate, prince of night.
I've been able to listen to your bones' misplacement,
particles of lime to feed the raven,
ligaments of torpor and vigilance resisting
the lunatic's brutal wallop and squawk: never more.
I can see your darkened blood, your mouth blue
from time and that deaf heart where shadow
was the filament of a thousand years of galleries and enclosures.
I have been able to watch your country of foam and the foliage
that covers your most beloved dreams
as if you still lived in that privileged place.

iv

Come along, come with me to hear the laughter of sorrows.
Let us look at the children's celestial map.
One must engineer phrases for your island, amnesiac stones
installed with the harness of the faded ones.
Don't allow the sea to diminish in its own unspoken secret.
No, Robinson. History is something else.
It is a hole in the mouth of nobody.
The nothingness we all know is part of our nonsense.
Evening will always be poised on the tip of the tongue,
a sunlit insult where pelicans and seagulls
dispute the thirst of whoever refuses to admit
the ant's victory over the soil.
Dawn's sweet proposals.
The world, the entire world is a black sphere,
a dreadful stain to destroy a shadow,
that old she-wolf guarding our wound.
I am not mistaken when I say that the word grace
incites laughter in lonesome men.

I have heard them and among them
you have crossed out amazement's finest salt
with a simple song, an absurd cooing
or a muddled plan to be an adventurer.
But for what? From which of this life's shores?
Nobody has granted you permission and you
have taken those black suns
as if they were part of your life,
the foolishness of a thought
that will never be extinguished.

v

Listen, listen to time's detonations.
Don't confuse the aviator's signs
with booming that begins on the tongue.
Powerful provocations. Time of scales.
Skin's filth and stubble.
And at the beach?
People constantly dock in other abysses.
They emerge. They split up. They do what they may.
Allow for a dispelled spirit's murmurs
to return to you as shells to sand.
There will be neither frogs nor luminaries like fierce Ulysses.

Tap-tap-tap
goes the sound of the sky's falling tears.
Panic's labyrinth lost
between your tongue's alphabets.
Tap: that disagreement with the animals
crossing the border.

Tap: days to come and those gone by,
terminal waters of a youngster
astonished in the sun's first light.
Tap: sounds of dresses falling at the drinking fountains
of the fugitive and friends.
Tap: tiny particles that crack
in a metal and emerald sky.
Tap: that castle of truth and thought
built from the saliva of sluggish mares.
Tap: the catafalques and apiaries where crazies cry
alongside widows stalemated by war.

Leave now, Robinson, leave your lair.
Sail different oceans where you may ply
through the serenity of a clear forecast.

vi

All of them are already gone. Your companion
with blue ibis feathers and your dog.
The erotic seashell open to your island's purity,
your carriage of dreams and its cotton landscapes,
the trains that shine even in the dark.

Now leave your silence and that tree growing immense
in its transparency. No consequence
will be the measure of a new world,
your whales' ecstatic castle.
There is no greater poem than the blue graveyard of beauty.
If you return here you'll see the shape of another century.
The brief interval that dilates the hours of our bones.
Remember that the size of death is never the same
its space is always in the awful stammering
that we are all bound to hear.

You will long for the time when a palm and its creaking
were a bonfire, that true pulse
that announced your home to you. And the always
trembling air would surprise you with its salty, tropical
breath, its burning love in earthly passion.
Distant dawns. Parts of the sun in your throat.
Birds from other heavens that you considered
siblings and friends, lavish glow of a log
and insect emancipations. Tree bark.
Amputations of lime among seaside plants.
Spells. And that crazy star that prefigured
the bouts between your head and heart.
Such delirium.

Someone broke the rope of your planet's light.
It will not be vision that goes with you
like drumbeats publicizing dawn.
That is vertigo: to stand alone and survey
a paradise at the edge of memory.

vii

Who remains? Who do you leave behind your yellowed atlas
when you go? Your parasol and hat. Vine on the hill
like a victory of your new century. Small goat
like a whisper that corresponds to your desire.
You await your incredible city full of echoing voices.
Its constituents don't register in your memory, they don't quake
for you, they don't protect you. Slow now are the angry pages
where alone they scrub their pornography.
You'll find no trace of them in a raindrop. No trace.
Now all of us people, holes without memory,
would live below ground looking in the subsoil for a word,
perhaps a fragment of fortune to allow us to speak
openly about a secret syllable.
This war and the sea's overwhelming saltpeter are strange.
And not ours. Insects nourished by someone else's substance.
They imitate a dry leaf's rare perfection. They consume.
There are larvae and nymphs. They bore a hole in the tree
for their young. Shims. Extensions. Parts of a faith

with rotten roots. They expand. They consume a portion
of an apocryphal paradise. And are sustained. They eat with
    pleasure.
They are nourished by meat and fresh fruit. Then the sea
comes to rest far from dreams. And echoes.
Open the door: use your hands to untie
the fields and flower gardens, the blue forests of tamarinds.
The bee will come and steal your knife.
The tapir will come to lick your wound.
The eagle will come to remove your light
and you will lose your regal head, ruler of your own blunder.

viii

Don't let anyone tell you what to do. Stand guard at the exits
of your indulgence. White termite mounds for your desire's salt.
Ample obstacles. Sacraments.
Thorny chains of suffering gather in your visions'
endless embrace. Have no fear. There will always be a good day
to speak with the wave and with the foam, with the fish that design
battles in which a reptile hides in the mud.
Stupidity and madness for whoever uses someone else's
keyboard to compose music. Renditions of laughing cats
calling upon tile roofs. Wailing.
No tiger exists to secure your suspicion. There is no fire.
Demand the thirst that cuts stones and hieroglyphs at dawn.
Saturn in your notebook.
Now there is no gold to saturate your heart. There's nothing.
The blue is intense. You can't distinguish
the void's southern region.
Pale salt auctions
on a castaway's skin. Save the land.

I listen to dawn's arrangements
in the soft beating of its moans.
And you go on still alone. You no longer dream.
It's enough for you to create secret webs
from earth's ephemeral buds. You adjust.
You allow fever to cover your roots. And you keep on.
Within your speech the ocean gently stirs.
The century passes beyond you. It is the sign,
the first sign of your ghosts. Who follows you?
Narrator of big promises I have seen you rouse dawn
from beneath the mollusk's useless creaking. Which moment
of desperation was yours? How many earthly complaints
did you gather among praise's flexible folds?

ix

Thirst grinds against public opinion.
Your anonymous and submissive public.
Omens of a faith that gets the better of bullies.
You open the hypocrite's skin one flake at a time
on a bed of algae. Old literary passages
leak like juice from a polyp.
A face improvises with its thousand radiant disguises.
The old man who offers you a foot massage walks by,
in your tracks and your shoes of lime and song
that always perforate the future's mirror
with a face. Depositions. Crusts.
Coatings of salt and signs. Green declarations
of the world and its renunciations. Horoscopes.
Kites of smoke. Foam lifting the air
of restless fish, fish of light
that wait in your dreams.
Your home left behind in the battle.
Half of paradise forgotten

like an extinguished torch.
You melt gold on a snowy road. And you use it up.
You guard a mountain's treasure. You're a catalyst
gathering and congregating the laypeople of the land.
Red ants in pilgrimage to your cave.
You itch as your saliva's joy
inflames your story's beginnings.
You're the precise owner, joy's perfect geometrician,
campesino anxious to see his rock,
eagle's shriek at the sacrifice of its daughters.
You have seen twelve revolving doors collapse. The moss that
    might
have revived your hills is gone. Now the earth hides its crazy,
greedy tasks, braiding laurel into the stillness of morning.
You decide to arrange your goat's intestines around your neck.
You simulate a night of openhearted love.
Birds sing to you.
Your memory is the country of sinister shadows.

XIV

We will never know paradise
with its peaks covered in violets
and its hills overcome
by the goldfinch's song,
we will never hear the sound
of skylights in water
that herald with a roar
the thicket's clarity,
there will never be a deep valley,
a cliff, a crag
that distills the greasy poison
of who we never were,
a sheep free and easy on the road,
we will never know petals adorning wreaths
nor fresh herbs budding by the shore,
nor those ripe vines,
defenseless temples of restrained fury
in the fog's highest caverns,
nor a thousand parrots dancing impulsively
in a southern forest while an old train

rusts in the dark station
of dry violins.
The dead will not sing
in a country that burns
beneath birch trees,
nor will the hundreds of embattled birds
that search for the laborer's
skinless brow day after day,
there will be no boiling noise of seeds
that announce the first rainfall
which arrived at the roots
where the son and his curiosity blindly go forth.
We will wait with clear, flowerlike eyes
for that future moment
when our house may be consumed
by a dispersed tribe's matrix
and the liturgy of a sun wandering in the winter
of that hasty, spellbound act,
that instant of truth
when life begins for us.

XV

And we will descend to other violent rivers
fertilizing pastures and vineyards, astral fields
where white coral becomes laughter
and by a colt's escape into open air
we will softly dream within borders, ire,
hardwood logs, bulls goring men,
and we will nail the bark of trees and bushes
with the twig, the edge, the rough stem
running its course to a dry field
beneath suns and stars with a gentle desire
to become girls running heartless
through open air, body to body, wet
and stale, the dazzling waves
of such a history, the timeless ones, of the eye
that found and watched a mythical, towering pueblo.
And now, countering years, cracks,
full, fortunate and chosen repetitions,
we will be able to distinguish those
who could be the cosmic monster,
the seam or ship destroyed by us,

as it was, after all, just a slip
and tumble in the grass.

XVI
(Sky Cycle)

i

A corrosive sky burns in my eyes.
Death is all its metaphors.
Its voice is the storm's intensity,
thunder at the lunatics' party.
The thread of consolation and desertion falls,
the light's water falls between birds,
the lover falls and the hater falls,
the distinctive one who smiles
before the foam of abyss. Goose feathers
collapse the labyrinth.

Whoever barks at a worm's ruddy mystery,
whoever destroys time with movement's rhythm,
whoever throbs before a cross of transparent fire,
where silence implores dawn's colors
in the throat of a sun lost in our childhoods.

A whirlpool begins in the blue tomb
of the unburied, and depicts the sage's youth
and the unhappy executioner's thirst against dream.
I expect nothing of God and his knives,
nothing of the stormy and irrational fire,
I know nothing of the peace that shatters decay.

All that burns here is the eager and bloody
ambition of what asks for death
without speaking of life.
The sky is a chiseled stone,
is a span of centuries in words,
dust saturated with blood,
the blood that embraces us at night.

The mercury sky burns,
it's air that brings about the vision of whoever digs,
it's a wandering road in infancy's silence,
it's a blinded voice, a fearful dream
of a relaxed mouth spitting out the blood
of an anthologized heart.
The sky here has caught up to us,
it's the exact hour where light
dims and the clouds rise by themselves
to illustrate distance.
The sky is each wall,
it's the grain of sand that bursts
and falls in the eye's brilliance like a poplar burning
dangerously in dawn's drunkenness.

(As children we sometimes keep
Sinbad's roar with us in bed.)

Now death is painted on stained glass,
like the cry of a man surrounded by piping,
like the same fire's blue crime,
like the history of the heart
of a man without memory.

ii

The sky is in my eyes.
I have fallen silent before the hurricane of its proverbs,
the jaws of thirst rising
from cracks in the mud.
I have fallen silent.
I have fallen silent before the men and children
and women hidden
like crude birds in invisible cloaks.
I have felt the shame of being someone
in my own words.
To live in ash inseparable
from filth and extermination,
to accept time covered in mold,
sullen time, time in the throat
that officiates the vertigo
of sacrilege and solitude between its cries.
I have lost the grace of tears in emptiness.
The emptiness of stupidity

and of expression and the suggestive lights
of the soldier in his ghostly exhaustion.
Emptiness of my benevolent feelings
among those who save trees
and mountains and the fleeting atmosphere
in the pain of confusion.
In my eyes I now preserve
a plaza of invisible dead leaves,
of cowardly parishioners
headlong in uncertainty,
of day after day in which
abysmal thirst conspires,
where a grave is home and a child's
shiny marble is an image.
And I think of expressions and shadows
and loyal dogs happy
to guard a bone on the road,
I think about the young woman who finds a place for old pans
in the limbo of a dream that would never expire,
in the air and its incoherent voice and the feverish rain
that visits our vitreous residence,
in the discovery of a bird plucked at dawn
and the sobbing of a man
trying to drown his image in a river,
in the ruin of a deserted room
of red velvet for the parties
of a girl and her fangs,
in the request of a dusty curtain
where an old woman crams herself
into absence that offers to leave one with nothing,

into the moon that punctually sets and scares children,
into the refuge of a word spoken in emptiness,
into the lost son's lethal courage
and to recover hope's eyes,
the fortunate mire of oblivion.

iii

I think of the fish and its calm happiness
traveling through a pool before its ruin,
in hollows and gullies
by the scarlet night's ascent,
in streams of blood and rivers
of blood, in the month's blood
and the blood of everyday.
Blood and its defeated dog fear,
blood and its cocky suicide dance,
blood and its adolescent anxiety,
blood with its leaves of light and horse,
that goes skyward and freezes in the stained glass,
the gothic, sickly, nostalgic and admired,
the one that spreads out its crazy costume,
its nocturnal salt, its procession of turkey flambé,
of relaxed sycophant on the train of origin,
promised comfort in the syringe
lulled asleep in the pail that buttresses tomfoolery,

blood that is one and all and forever
of street of tree of Icarus with his vacant eyes,
of Sappho and the sores of Catullus,
of the Aegean and its house of wind
and its silenced deceit of wind,
of blue-eyed Libya
and adulterous Juvencio
and little girl Venus
and Lesbia's love
and meretricious Mamurra
and sickly Caesar
and an earful from sexy Cato
and the beating Nonnus gave Vatinius
and don't die Helios for no light is greater
than blood from a wound, blood
that escapes from your face.
And there is not enough blood
to cure the world of the world.
The world that even after it is the world
embraces this world.
And Castor and Pollux appear lost against the sky
with a hunger for blood that slakes their blood
and where blood remains I will keep searching.

iv

The sky is in my eyes,
it is a weariness fallen from God's pen
and books, a peasant's extermination
and a grief stricken land's harsh tone,
frail before children and the children's silence.
Sky falls from sky into air
with the serenity of a mountain compelled
by its thistles' slow howl,
it is the flight wed since childhood to a thrush
secluded in an airplane's solitude.
I came here, to dream that the world
was one and was all and that its voice leaked
sounds that are suited to the dark.

I can pummel the world with my strength,
I can push against the injustice of thought,
I can lick the blood
of a broken statue in a foggy wasteland,

I can feel my legs and my arms
in my gun-toting city of fire,
frozen in daybreak's dream.

I can believe there is a page
that is not written by God
and God's pirates.
It's my own page in the book of nobody.

It's a leaf from a tree that breathes
like a dead shard.
It's a prayer to say during the plunge,
my voice's urgency, daughter of Minerva,
last of my kind,
now I can end this intolerable life,
this life of salt that smells like a dry reservoir.
I can paint the name I've forgotten
on that blank page,
with the terror and fear
of having seen a foreign butcher
with gravedigger eyes. I know that I can.

I will have to enlighten myself with a black tear.

v

The sky is in my body.
It exists in me with the comfort a root
gives the mud. And it centers me.
It assembles all my organs, illuminates
my veins two by two, unsettles the source
of narrow drafts that pass through my belly
and chokes on the friendly pulse the grips me.
My body is its shelter.
It's a resonant place accustomed
to everything in silence that interrupts,
admits, stalks, waits at the doorway of my being
and provokes me.

The sky, the whole sky, is in my body.
In me it becomes a second fog,
membrane of terrible weather
in which men request an audience
with the winged wind, with the dark lip of the dead.

It makes of itself this road,
obeys the generous movement's
sacrilegious noise,
lying supine on pavement like the masses
so that the body might recover
the abysmal scepter of its ashes.
At the threshold of smoke it approaches.
it opens so the sea hushes its strange
anonymous voice,
its will to be that stowed-away being.

The century fills its silence.
It's a flower garden where birds squawk,
where in water's confines
trash is the alphabet deciphered by
those who live in the victory of days.

The sun sings its mud psalm.
It's a chant for dead waters,
for the asylum of the sick and history's
pustules and dry tongue,
it's the guardian's exile in the company of a slave
when the angels fall
into the salt of junkyards,
fall into the flame's narrow defeat.

The century, this century, has already abandoned us.
It has renounced us.

It rains on the century, it rains
on young bodies and old souls,
on the decline of roofs seeking land
and cold columns in vacant lots,
it rains a shabby agreement between tempests.
It rains on frontiers of other languages, isolated races
where servants to lies and disgrace
are dead rats in an anonymous emissary's potion,
it rains on borders where a pilgrim practices magic,
on mutinous nights before the Father's indictment,
in the age of the captive splayed against stone walls,
in the loneliest cave underground,
on maritime shells and hot ashes
where a sailor's vomit went overboard.

It rains on the open text without an author,
it rains on fire and burns,
it rains on the house and burns,
it rains on water and burns,
it rains on dreams and burns
like an animal devastated by routine.

vi

There is an ecstasy in the gloomy water
that sends its crazy dismantled song
flowing through the city's streets,
that city of dust and sorrow,
of chronicles and newspapers,
beat down by a caustic donkey's feverish meditation
and assorted luteless, boneless beasts.
In the past my city flew within my mind's grasp,
it was a small place where fairies and magicians
brewed their aquatic spell.
My city was a party for the lizard and its caution,
for the scorpion, trustee of purity's stench,
on an open path to intoxication.

Its crosses of ash filter into pitchers.
Its fish are the dream where the squalid and crazy dance.
Its sunlids set on its acid tongue.
Its chest, its ears, sing to the age of revenge.

Its dawn vertebrae are vertebrae of life.
Its legs are made of air, its mouth of fallen rust.
Its pugilist hand, its naval is whistling pages.
Its blank paper of brittle teeth burns.
Burning is its bible plastic,
forgotten belt of absentees,
burning in the infinity of its old age and poverty.
Its sibilline flies lick its ink's crazy course.
Its cave birds piss on laughter.
Its swarming birds are shoreline fish.
Its leaden birds vomit fever petals,
its foam vertigo, its immaterial moon,
its sistrum like a body in a tragedy
abandons its orphans' sterile cavity.
Its rifle name breathes in agony.
Its streets are blasphemies, its lamps
the rhythm of warning from cyclopean lightning.

This city of mine is an open remainder, a root
that runs through my veins, a glimmer of sun
pursuing of its tongue's luxury, a cave
where Sinbad sings to Ali Baba
of the sea's final plotless dream.

Its promises are hidden in whitewashed coffins.
There is a long avenue made of air
that shelters all its garbage.
Rats live there in mankind's feast,
in compassion's slow adulation.
Its mouth spits up the homeless, its eternity

is the pavement's lime and song. Its assiduous clarity
is a racket, a scar open to greed.
If only my city could recoup the cost of its fables.
Perhaps if the espousal
of a sultan and his princess or an eternal story
in its crystal and gold rags could protect it
from that impure word, blue since the beginning
that little by little annihilates it and chokes it, innocent
of the place where deaf chickens are slaughtered.

Perhaps if it were a Byzantine circus,
an emerald-encrusted scabbard, a hidden dungeon
for guarding a cadaver's dust and the pulleys
of its dust hallucinations, perhaps.

And in the mirror of salt and promises
where faces abandon its unique tragedy
I can see it exhausted and defenseless
with its mantel of weddings fallen to ruin,
with its dirty life and its insignificant victories
with the courage of an obsequious servant
and of a hen that passes through my throat.

I've decided to love it like this, in the indecent
hours of its begging.

vii

The sky is in my eyes.
It's a nomad's dream in a fervor
of rains taken by the soul.

The sky is a horse
trotting across the horizon,
a homeless eagle's vertigo,
breathless rooster's open crow,
an astronomically speedy guffaw.
Its dream is a crack
in the crawdad's blue skull,
a plume's plea to daytime's scythe,
atomic upheaval of its phantoms.
Its dream is a cup, a pot
in a broken kitchen's majesty
when life's splendid imagination radiates
with the aroma of a bundle of herbs and its flies.

The sky dreams a dream that scratches at
a thousand and one meters of mud and its debts
when the earth transforms into decomposed
bones, crumbs of a world in arms
surrounded by darkness. It records the figures
of its terrestrial declaration, of seams
and cartridges, of maps and hemispheres,
of deceptive herbs and dry sticks
in its earthworms' synthesis,
cadavers and more cadavers
in its bullets' burning outback.
Salt cadavers for the girl god of its fables,
so that everything will be, so that nothing ends
so that the bullet will remain
in its scattered demons.

Among the animals a pig ignites,
exhaling its perfume in an ecstatic groan
and white mutations. The cats' mouths
are a deep cry in sweet nightmares
that illuminate night in a celestial garden.
The daybreak's bandages and its lust
are now legends for blocking bridges,
shipwrecks and the rasping of a land
that once accommodated centaurs
and green poseidons in its stories.
The sun's skins wither away.
There are gusts of smoke made into smoke,
tress that insinuate smoke
between stones and buckets,

there's smoke of being smoke to be smoke
in the foliage and it multiplies
the freshness of smoke, too much smoke
in cries and shots
"and come back to the eyes and shut up to the moon,"
say the old women in the remote forest of smoke.

viii

The sky is my frontier.
It is my claim of salt and paradise
beneath the castaway's motionless eyelids.
I have arrived at this moment when dawn
was the right distance to bring me near the other:
that adolescent despot that I was in the moss,
in the sun's gentle rumor beneath walls.
Did someone say my name beneath the profane
law of silence?
How many streets did I feed
with fire? Who cut the sick and defenseless
rose for the final member of the tribe?

I was the sorrow of shell and of fire
when in the temple the caricatures of God
were the graceful lamb of crime. I was
on this bamboo fence when the first
and last idea was to pull the fingernails

and teeth from the vulture's imagination.
The unlikely vulture with its message of war.
Each moment of dawn, each instant of aurora
was meeting a throbbing reflection
between swamps of fear
beneath a red sun that roared and marched
in the eardrum of hollow men.
The straw men that inhabit the poem,
those without anything, the sane of the procession
and the abyss, angels of virtue and menace,
parents of hell's lobby.

Dante wouldn't have hesitated to sketch them
on the border with their brilliant skin of bitter fish.
Then it was my infancy
and I had hardly a thousand and one years
of walking in that bonfire,
of awaiting the dove's coffins,
the temple of Ephesus and Homer's superstition.

A thousand and one years of being a girl
on the old paths of fever
and understanding. Everything seemed immense.
There were sabers as fast as dream
and a liturgy of canticles and masses for the heretic
and his pulpit of geese in the entrails
of the sane.
Stains on the equation of paradise,
pustules and ruins in the tree's friendship,
small lichen

for the delighted passage of a time
in which our lives meant something,
perhaps only the vertigo
of disenchantment.

ix

Sounds of shrapnel fill the air around the buildings.
A layer of dust and ivory
traces the child's imagination.
And his head howls and shakes
in the darkness of thought.

At that time I was small
and didn't know how to go on until the end. I waited.
I saw women passing in morning's
lethargy, in the street's water troughs
where we, along with the sky's blue ray,
we were a chorus of fireflies with five senses
set in the wind's breath.
I waited.
I believed beauty was a lonely life's fire.
Water was the lookout's voice while someone
stole cadavers, ink skeletons,
earthen bodies already lacking biography.

There were green birds in emerald palaces.
Multicolored birds
for night's blank dreams.
Fountains covered in visions and a nightingale
that sadly sings to the prince in his charade.

The future was a merciless pen in prisons.
Time blushed for time and us,
beneath the echo's gratitude, we had thousands
of secure years on pages of mud and salt,
humble navigations without return . . .

It was a noisy world and its silent movement,
its tailless spirit and terror anointed by the wind
of an infancy stuck to death's vapor.
At some point in time we all had this dream of returning
and having life renewed, the flower of erosion
in the word and the universe in the hand of one race.

When were we whom? Where do we leave what?
Because the time of salt was the grimace of knowing
that nobody was never and that we were never
the unfamiliar voice of nothingness,
only a multitude of remote caves, of failed
virgins and gestures that resist and defeat you.
And you call yourself a staunch father,
uncertain father that fades
and denies himself when someone asks
his name in a hospital's labyrinth.

I said goodbye to you, you no longer need us.
The century sinks tied to its halflight.
I'm leaving, city, I'm leaving
lit up and so dark is your color
that there is neither sky nor dream
from the crystal man.
Pity I ask of the glow
that flutters anonymously in my eyes,
that for you issues forth from Aladdin's mouth
and Hassan's barber.
Have pity astral city, lamp of the universe.
Take to court the deep water of abyss
and tell the king
that yours is the heart of mankind.

Remember there's always someone
who lies about your history
even as flashlights shine
into your life's holy hole.

XVII

I see you now, in your crust of light and song, at the earthy
limit of your stories, those furrows where your history
always departs as a disastrous ordeal.
I see and hear you as a fragment of truth
where time scrunches up, dissolves and then
grows to reach the shadow of that place we described.
And it's a street now with a downhill ditch,
the silence we pass through daily on the dusty road.
And it is time's small trick that introduces us
slowly to the mirror's back, where the world is a world
in your mouth and routine is in the realm of your dream.
And nothing suffices but the moon's furtive passage,
the beginning of an abrupt sky
where we are blind to someone,
perhaps a cry undone by silence,
a fallen scale at the end of our fiction.
It is not sufficient to have lived a little among such places,
places visited by laughter's admonition.
Our history was lost in the garden we visited
in childhood dreams, places of salt and song

where we believed we were captains of mud,
soldiers of some regiment that sustained the living.
Now we know we can dig up our days
along the wall of meetings
where we thought our friend was part of the charade.
The dead shark is still splayed out on the beach
like a stigmata of truth.
Now the sea wants to stitch its name
in heavenly patchwork. It wants to.
What's missing is the point on the page to create land.
And for the word to burn in the port
like a suburb of life. That's what's missing.